Piano • Vocal • Guitar

Jack Johnson
and Friends

Sing-A-Longs and Lullabies for the film
Curious George

ISBN-13: 978-1-4234-1316-5
ISBN-10: 1-4234-1316-4

HAL•LEONARD®
CORPORATION

7777 W. BLUEMOUND RD. P.O. BOX 13819 MILWAUKEE, WI 53213

Visit Hal Leonard Online at
www.halleonard.com

Contents

UPSIDE DOWN

Words and Music by
JACK JOHNSON

Moderate groove

Who's to ___ say ___ what's im-pos-si-ble? But

they for-got ___ this world keeps spin-nin'. And ___ with

D.S. al Coda

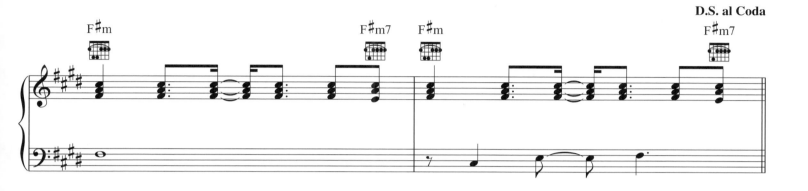

CODA

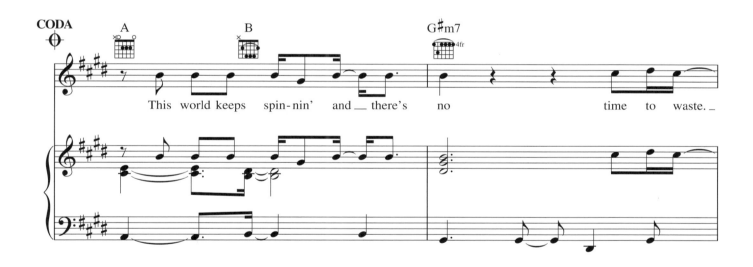

This world keeps spin-nin' and __ there's no   time to waste. __

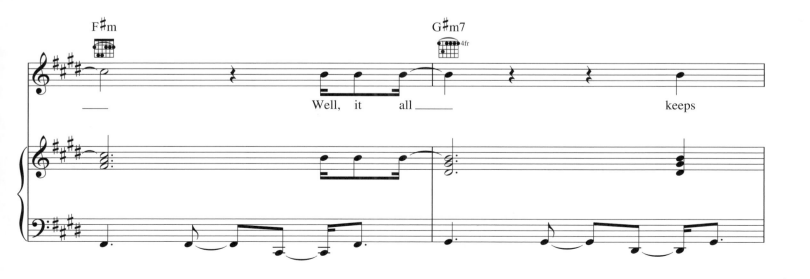

__ Well, it all _____   keeps

BROKEN

Words and Music by
JACK JOHNSON

side.

Said with-

out you I___ was bro-ken, but___ I'd rath-er be broke__ down with__ you by__ my

side.

1. I did-n't know what I was look-in' for, so I did-n't know what I'd find.
2. *(See additional lyrics)*

D.S. al Coda

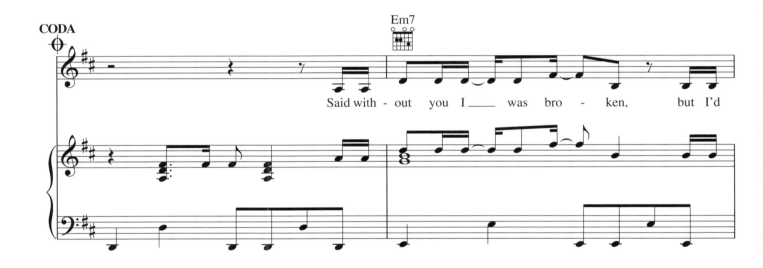

Said with - out you I ___ was bro - ken, but I'd

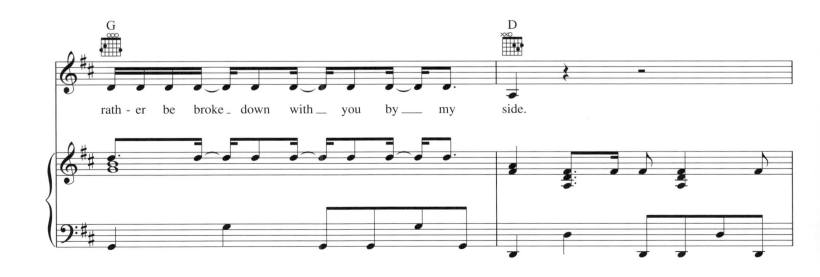

rath - er be broke _ down with ___ you by ___ my side.

Additional Lyrics

2. With everything in the past
Fading faster and faster until it was gone,
Found out I was losing so much more than I knew all along,
Because everything I've been working for
Was only worth nickels and dimes.
But if I had a minute for every hour that I've wasted,
I'd be rich in time, I'd be doing fine.

PEOPLE WATCHING

Words and Music by
JACK JOHNSON

lone - ly, lone - ly, lone - ly, lone - ly, lone - ly, lone - ly.

WRONG TURN

Words and Music by
JACK JOHNSON

TALK OF THE TOWN

Words and Music by
JACK JOHNSON

I wan-na be ___ where the talk of the town ___ is a-bout ___ last night ___ when the sun ___ went down. ___ Yeah, _____ and the trees ___ all dance ___ and the warm ___ wind blows ___ in that same ___ old ___

To Coda ⊕

- be it's as strange as it seems. __
- ways be as strange as it seems. __

Mm mm. __

And the trou - ble I find __ is that the

trou - ble finds me. __ It's a part of my mind, __ it be - gins __ with a dream __ and a

feel - ing I get __ when I look __ and I see __ that this world __ is a puz - zle. I'll

JUNGLE GYM

Words and Music by
GARRETT DUTTON

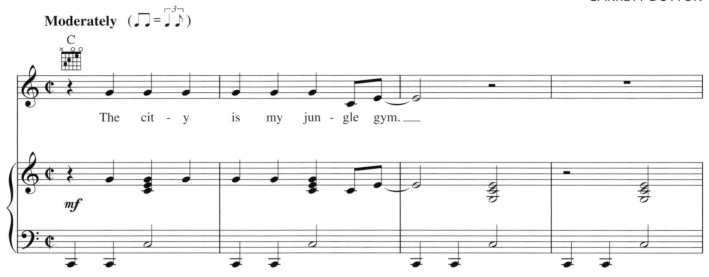

WE'RE GOING TO BE FRIENDS

Words and Music by
JACK WHITE

Moderately fast

Fall is here, _ hear the yell, _ back to school, ring the bell. _

Brand-new shoes, walk-ing blues, _ climb the fence, _ books and pens, _

I can tell that we are gon-na be friends. Yes,

SHARING SONG

Words and Music by ZACHARY GILL
and ADAM TOPOL

THE 3 R'S

Words and Music by BOB DOROUGH
and JACK JOHNSON

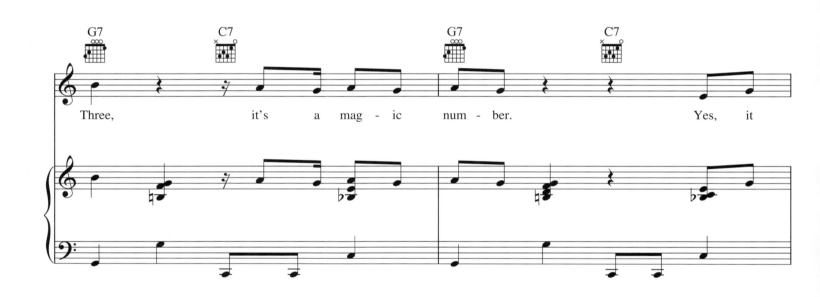

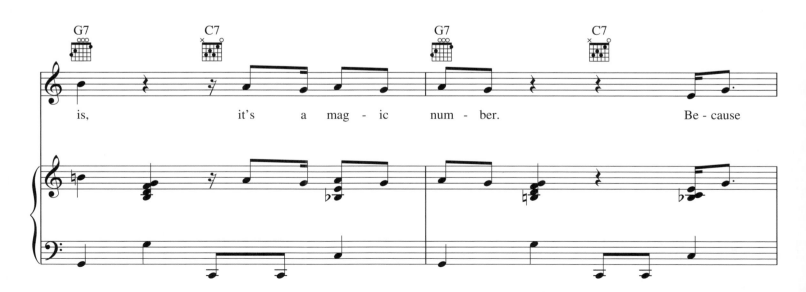

LULLABY

Words and Music by
MATT COSTA

Recorded a half step lower.

WITH MY OWN TWO HANDS

Words and Music by
BEN HARPER

QUESTIONS

Words and Music by
JACK JOHNSON

Ques - tions, _ I've got some ques - tions. _ I want to
pres - sions, _ you've made im - pres - sions. _ They're go - ing

know _ you, _ but what if I could ask you on - ly one thing _ on - ly this
no - where. _____ They're just gon - na wait here if you let them. _ Please _ don't

one time, _ what would you tell _ me? _ Well, may - be you could give me a sug -
let them. _ I want to know _ you. _ And if they're gon - na haunt me, please col -

Recorded a half step lower.

SUPPOSED TO BE

Words and Music by
JACK JOHNSON

Maybe it's up with the stars, _____
Maybe it's trapped in a jar, _____

maybe it's under the sea,
something we've already seen.

maybe it's not very far. _____
Maybe it's no-where at all. _____

May-be